ETHEREUM

Complete Guide to Ethereum And The Blockchain Technology, Ethereum Mining, Smart Contracts, And Decentralized Applications

MATT COHEN

Copyright © 2017 Matt Cohen - All rights reserved.

In no way is it legal to reproduce, duplicate, or transmit any part of this document in either electronic means or in printed format. recording of this publication is strictly prohibited and any storage of this document is not allowed unless with written permission from the publisher. all rights reserved. The information provided herein is stated to be truthful and consistent, in that any liability, in terms of inattention or otherwise, by any usage or abuse of any policies, processes, or directions contained within is the solitary and utter responsibility of the recipient reader. under no circumstances will any legal responsibility or blame be held against the publisher for any reparation, damages, or monetary loss due to the information herein, either directly or indirectly. Respective authors own all copyrights not held by the publisher. The information herein is offered for informational purposes solely, and is universal as so. the presentation of the information is without contract or any type of guarantee assurance. The trademarks that are used are without any consent, and the publication of the trademark is without permission or backing by the trademark owner. all trademarks and brands within this book are for clarifying purposes only and are the owned by the owners themselves, not affiliated with this document. The author wishes to thank these sources for the images of this book: ethereum.org (CC-BY), Draglet, 99bitcoins.com, coinbase.com. Unless specified differently, all the images are released under Creative Commons CC-BY-SA License.

MATT COHEN

TABLE OF CONTENTS

Free Bonus: Make Money Online - 5 Proven And Legitimate Ways To Earn Money From Your Computer	7
Introduction	11
Chapter 1: What I sEthereum	13
Chapter 2: The Future of Ethereum	18
Chapter 3: Ethereum Virtual Machine	22
Chapter 4: The Ethereum Enterprise Alliance	24
Chapter 5: Ethereum Investments	28
Chapter 6: Mining Ether on Ethereum	36
Chapter 7: Ethereum Smart Contracts	40
Chapter 8: Programming with Ethereum	52
Chapter 9: Problems You May Run into with Ethereum	54
Chapter 10: Tips and Tricks for Using Ethereum	58
Chapter 11: The Ethereum Ecosystem	62
Chapter 12: Buying Ethereum	64
Chapter 13: Ethereum Milestones	68
Chapter 14: Smart Contract Myths	70
Conclusion	74
Other Books By Matt Cohen	76

MATT COHEN

FREE BONUS
MAKE MONEY ONLINE - 5 PROVEN AND LEGITIMATE WAYS TO EARN MONEY FROM YOUR COMPUTER

The majority of people thinks earning an income through the internet is just a dream, or alternatively some sort of scam. However, there are many legitimate ways to earn money from your computer.

In this short guide you're about to discover 5 proven ways you can follow to actually start making money online, for real. Each one comes with a rating based on 3 factors:

- How quick can you actually earn your first dollar? (5 stars = really quick)
- Is it easy for a beginner with little to no previous experience? (5 stars = really easy)
- Is it cheap to start or does it require a high investment? (5 stars = really cheap or free)

Go to **www.eepurl.com/c5Ybb1** to download the free guide.

MATT COHEN

INTRODUCTION

Congratulations on downloading *Ethereum: Complete Guide to Ethereum and the Blockchain Technology, Ethereum Mining, Smart Contracts, and Decentralized Applications* and thank you for doing so.

The following chapters will discuss the technology behind Ethereum.

You may not know much about Ethereum, but you may know about bitcoin. Ethereum is not going to be much different from bitcoin since they are both going to be blockchain applications. However, you will have more options when it comes to investing in the platform.

This book will give you all of the information that you need to make an informed decision on if you want to invest with Ethereum or not.

Ethereum is a platform that will allow you to trade a digital currency that is also going to make it to where you can write outsmart contracts so that you are not having to worry about spending a lot of money.

One of Ethereum's biggest goals is to save its users money, and from what you will notice in this book, you will see that they will be doing just that. You are not only going to be saving money, but you will be getting rid of outside variables that could end up messing up your investments.

Another great thing that you will notice is that Ethereum is not going to require a lot of money to invest, unlike the stock market.

There are plenty of books on this subject on the market, thanks again for choosing this one! Every effort was made to ensure it is full of as much useful information as possible; please enjoy!

CHAPTER 1
WHAT IS ETHEREUM

Ethereum's blockchain is public, programmable, and even decentralized. Ethereum provides a peer to peer contract as it allows you to mine and trade ether, the platform's cryptocurrency token. You will be surprised to know that Ethereum was not proposed until the year 2013 by a Russian Canadian engineer that worked with bitcoin. Taking his inspiration from bitcoin, Vitalik Buterin used it to create Ethereum. His idea was to create a blockchain that would exceed bitcoin. However, it was not until the following year that Ethereum got the funding that it needed to begin the development process.

The official logo of the Ethereum platform

It was during the creation process that developers decided that Ethereum was going to go beyond bitcoin's peer to peer system and would have more services to offer its users than bitcoin. However, there were questions that came up about the scalability and the security that Ethereum had to offer. These are still two of the most prominent issues that the users of Ethereum have. As Ethereum was being developed, it won the World Technology Award in 2014.

The live blockchain was launched in July of 2015. At first, the program was developed by the Ethereum Switzerland GmbH and the Ethereum foundation. It was in spring of the next year that ether was established, and its net worth was one billion dollars. A website by the name of Vox said: "Ethereum is a new digital currency and is a challenge to bitcoin because of the wide range of services that bitcoin was unable to provide."

There are a lot of people that do not know that there are more cryptocurrencies than Ethereum and bitcoin. However, why do you want to choose Ethereum over any other cryptocurrency? Below you will see the good and the bad of Ethereum so that you can make an informed decision on if you want to invest with Ethereum now or sometime in the future.

Your contract will be executed as you state it to be

Many times, when a contract is written, a lawyer has to look at it, and a judge has to enforce it. This will be an expensive process. So, Ethereum offered smart contracts as a way to provide a cheaper contract solution. The smart contracts will be governed by the distributed autonomous organization.

Because of the distributed autonomous organization, you are not going to have to worry about how your contract is written or if it will be carried out as you want it to be. Each contract will be required to work inside of the DAO's rules. This way both parties involved in the contract are protected.

Because of the DAO, there is not going to be any need for judges or lawyers to be involved in your contract process. At the same time, you need to make sure you are rereading your contract before you are sending it to the system. A trustless operations system has never been established; but, Ethereum is using the way that technology evolves to attempt to create one.

Distributed Autonomous Organization

Digix was funded by five million in ether so that another cryptocurrency called dapp could be created. This cryptocurrency is backed by gold which makes it different than any other cryptocurrency. Dapp's funding was raised in one day. Thanks to the funding, it was able to start the company right away without having to wait for the financing. Once they started their business, they were able to create a board that determined how tokens would be distributed and various other things that would require someone to make the decision. This took investors, banks, and lawyers out of the equation. While for investors being left out of the equation is not fun, it does take some stress off of them because it is terrifying to invest in a company that they do not know what will happen with them.

The DAO will take the options that are required for the contract and simplify them into a single layer, so developers and users have an easier time in working on the platform.

Little costs

Being that Ethereum works off the DAO, it will eliminate costs that will be associated with business functions due to the fact that they will be done automatically. This is mostly due to the fact that you are not going to have to purchase an office building as you will see later on in this section.

EtherEx will provide you with a decentralized system that will have a cryptocurrency that is trustless. The EtherEx will work on an infrastructure that is similar to Digix where there will be a group of people that make important decisions. This board and the foundation have assisted in reducing the gas cost for a nonprofit organization.

What it comes down to is that when a business is built on a DAO, Ethereum will reduce the cost of setting up a building. You are no longer going to have to have your own building or buy office supplies for your employees to use. There will still be a small cost that will come with using the DAO. However, that cost is not going to be nearly as much if you had to rent your own building and all of the supplies. On top of it, you will have an unlimited number of employees working for you since they will be working remotely.

Still new

Sadly, Ethereum is still new, and it will continue to be developed so that their users can hopefully have a platform that can offer them anything that they could possibly want. When you compare Ethereum and bitcoin, you will see that bitcoin is more established, but it cannot provide what Ethereum can offer.

Legal advice

Ethereum has gotten rid of the need to involve judges and lawyers in your contracts. This can be good because you will be saving money. But, you have to know how the system works to ensure that you are making a decision that will be the best for you. The only thing you will have to worry about is that computers will have flaws, so a human has to be there to ensure that the platform and its code are running efficiently.

Changes

With the system always updating you will have to deal

with the system shutting down so that it can apply those updates. The servers can also end up being overloaded which will cause them to shut down without warning. The evolving is not always a bad thing, but it will be if you are working on a deadline and you are not able to meet your deadline.

Remote employees

Since you will have employees that are not going to be working where you can keep an eye on them, you will have to deal with them being in different time zones and even with them being distracted by their personal life. It is not going to be too different than if your employees were working in an office building. So, make sure that you understand what is going on with your employees so that you can better prepare for what they will be dealing with as they work for you.

Competition

One of the biggest things that you will have to deal with is competition. There may not be enough competition, but if that happens, then you will be around for very long. But, when there are too many people on Ethereum then you will have a lot of people to fight against when it comes to mining pools.

There will be plenty of good things that will come from using Ethereum just like there will be bad things. But, you cannot stop that from using Ethereum. Ethereum is using technology and evolving to create an entirely new world of digital currency. You never know what will happen with Ethereum as it is changing and you will be part of history when you use Ethereum.

Take the good with the bad and figure out if Ethereum will be the platform you to invest in or not. If you can get past the bad and move on to the good, then you will be able to invest with Ethereum without any worry.

MATT COHEN

CHAPTER 2
THE FUTURE OF ETHEREUM

Just like every other piece of technology, you are not going to know the future and what it will do. Ethereum is a platform that will offer you more than bitcoin, and that makes it to where it will have the possibility of outlasting bitcoin.

Since Ethereum is continuously changing, it will run the risk of crashing and burning or continuing on as it has been. The evolution as you have seen is not always a bad thing, but it is something that can stand in the way of your investing with Ethereum. With the servers continually going down, you may find that you do not want to invest in something that is so unstable and is making it to where you are unaware if you will be able to do what you have to do on a day to day basis.

You will have to watch the news to ensure that you can tell what the market is doing so that you can figure out what is going on with the platform. Ethereum will be similar to investing in the stock market. It will have its ups and downs, and if you are unprepared for one of the falls, you will lose your coins.

If you invest with Ethereum, you will hold onto the hope that it will stick around so that you can continue to trade on the platform as well as mine coins.

Since blockchain is changing so many sectors in the world, is it possible that the blockchain applications will stick around longer than anyone can predict? Or, is the government going to find some way to step in and begin to govern them or get rid of them all together. Cryptocurrency is already subjected to tax therefore it is already monitored by the government. However, how far is the government going to be willing to go to tell you what you can and cannot do with your Ethereum cryptocurrency?

Unfortunately, no one can tell the future. Therefore no one will know what the future holds for Ethereum and other blockchain applications. One-minute Ethereum could be here, and the next minute it could be gone because of the government or because of traditional banking systems. There is no telling what will happen with Ethereum sadly, so you cannot say that it will stick around. However, you can look at how good it is doing and make an educated guess that it will stick around.

If you look at some of the cryptocurrencies that have already vanished, they vanished overnight. However, how do does anyone know what is to happen with the ones that appear to be stable?

If you were able to tell the future, the chances are that you will be able to see that Ethereum will still be around because of how much it has to offer its users. You have not seen a lot about Ethereum yet in this book, but you will see that Ethereum is a vital asset to those who are investing with digital currencies.

Maybe sometime in the future, Ethereum will open themselves up to other cryptocurrencies because they will want to make a more efficient platform and opening themselves up would be something that would not only help the Ethereum users but would help draw in users who use bitcoin and even litecoin.

There have not been any announcements as to what Ethereum has to offer its users lately, but there is probably going to be several projects in the works for Ethereum that they do not want the public to know about yet because they are wanting to ensure that the coding is just right before they release the projects for beta testing or any other further testing that will be required by the users.

MATT COHEN

CHAPTER 3
ETHEREUM VIRTUAL MACHINE

A virtual machine was put into place for Ethereum so that security could be taken care of whenever code that cannot be trusted is executed since this piece of code is executed by almost every computer in the world. Whenever you observe the virtual machine, you will realize that the virtual machine will work on Ethereum's security against attacks; more specifically DOS attacks that are directed at cryptocurrency platforms. The virtual machine is also going to make it to where external programs are not able to interfere with any communication points that are running the program.

The chances are that you are not a programmer, so you are not going to know what a DOS attack is let alone how to prevent them. Therefore, you need to understand what they are and how the virtual machine will stop them from attacking the Ethereum system.

Ethereum virtual machine will run off a runtime environment as smart contracts are executed. And, with how popular smart contracts are becoming by Ethereum users, it is possible that these smart contracts will take over the financial industry. However, the smart contract technology will complete tasks that have to be achieved without having supervision which makes it a version of machine learning.

A paper was written by Dr. Wood that stated that the virtual machine was created in a sandbox environment which means that it will have the ability to change the future of cryptocurrency because there is one piece of code that will outperform every other platform.

The sandbox environment is not going to be the ideal environment because you are not going to be able to see the program's full potential due to the fact that the initial states continuously change. Sandbox environments are not going to be like the real world where the users are because the users will use the program in a way that is different than how a computer will use it. But, testing the program in a sandbox environment is one of the safest ways that developers will be able to check the constraints of a program without releasing it to the public. This means they can ensure that the coding for the program is right and is not going to crash on the users thus causing the users to get upset and possibly leave the program for good.

While you watch the day to day operations on a decentralized system, you will know that the virtual machine will be what is in charge of making sure that those tasks are completed in the order that they are supposed to be completed in.

The best thing about the virtual machine is that it is free! This means that every programmer will download it and use it.

CHAPTER 4
THE ETHEREUM ENTERPRISE ALLIANCE

Fortune 500 companies, blockchain startups, and research groups got together in the spring of 2017 and started da nonprofit organization that is called the ethereum enterprise alliance. Some of the companies that are in the enterprise are Microsoft and Intel. There are at least a hundred and sixteen members that are part of the enterprise alliance.

The official EEA logo

This alliance was created as an open source for private blockchains that these companies are using. The blockchains will address the data that is stored in the blocks for every sector that is using blockchain, which means that everything from banking to entertainment is being used by these companies. The alliance has found a solution that addresses the ethereum ecosystem that is used by ethereum users, including the alliance. The technology that the alliance is creating is not only helping them achieve their goals, but it is making ethereum more efficient for everyone who uses it.

Some alliance members have announced that they are creating new projects on their blockchain. One of these projects is a hybrid architecture which will bridge private chains to public chains. The new blockchain will be public and will open up new possibilities that were not available before if it had not been for the company putting their project ideas into action.

The blockchain for ethereum is always changing which means that the information in the company's blockchain will be open for the public to see what the company is doing. So, at the end of the day, Ethereum Enterprise Alliance wants to open up private blockchains to free blockchains. When you open up the closed blockchains, what the businesses are doing is not going to be hidden anymore, and the public will see how they are operating from the inside. There may not be a way for the public to interact with the company, but that does not mean that the public is not going to be able to better understand enterprises. And, if the public can see everything, then how are the big fortune 500 companies going to be able to hide from their public when questions are asked about how their money is being used in creating a better experience for their customers.

One of the most significant sectors that wants to bridge the gap are the financial companies because they do not want to lose their customers. This is why they are wanting to join in with the blockchain technologies so that they can show their customers that they are willing to join in with the way that the future is going and continue to hold the trust of their customers.

It is always easier to understand when you can see that a company's ideas are actually put into action. So, let's look at a few companies that are working to put their ideas into action for the ethereum users.

    1. JP Morgan Chase started a blockchain that stood

between public and private blockchains so that payments could be sent and received. The inspiration came from a regulator that needed access to the transactions for their company while keeping their customer's privacy secure.
2. The Royal bank in Scotland announced that they were created a tool that would help clear out settlements on the distributed ledger. The ledger worked with smart contract technology and let users write out their settlement deals.

CHAPTER 5
ETHEREUM INVESTMENTS

Ethereum will be like Bitcoin where you can invest in it. Just as you saw earlier, the blockchain for both platforms will track the transactions. But, since Ethereum is still new, there will be differences that a user is not going to be able to that they were going to be able to do on the Bitcoin platform.

There are a lot of people who think that Ethereum will end up surpassing bitcoin due to the fact that it offers different services to its users and it has new developments and codes being put into its system. However, just like bitcoin, you can invest in the Ethereum platform and have access to the ether cryptocurrency as well as have the ability to exchange them with other users. So, why should you pick Ethereum to invest with? As you saw earlier, Ethereum is decentralized and will lower the risks of theft, fraud, and interferences. This means that you will be investing in a platform that has a whole new set of restraints that you are not going to find on bitcoin.

The first thing that you will need to do is to know how Ethereum works. Since Ethereum will work off contracts that will unlock payments when specific conditions are met. Take for example that person A will need to fulfill three algorithms before they are awarded their ether for the work that they have completed. This payment will be sent to them automatically and is not going to require another transaction unless that is stipulated in the contract. On top of that, ownership of the program can be transferred from user to user as long as the user is on the blockchain; so, this means that you will be able to trade contracts as well. Any transaction that is done with the autonomous agent, the program will make it so that deals do not need to be done with supervision. So, this makes Ethereum similar to a cloud service that will have the option of expanding and even renting out additional servers in the event that it is profitable for the user.

So, now that you understand how Ethereum works more let's look at the investment side of things. Just like you have seen already, ether is Ethereum's cryptocurrency just like bitcoin is for bitcoin. Ether is what is used in making the payments necessary for the transactions that are completed when a smart contract has had its conditions met. Ether is also going to validate the transactions while syncing new deals with the network so that everything is updated in real time.

Ether first started getting distributed in 2015 through a crowdfunding campaign that lasted over a month. There were at least sixty million dollars in the ether that was raised so that Ethereum could be developed further. To add to it, there were eighteen million dollars raised as well. This campaign was reported as the most prominent crowdfunding campaign in the history of the platform.

As you look at the investment opportunities that there are with Ethereum, it is equally as important to be able to assess the value of Ether. To do that, you must look at several different aspects such as:

- Cryptocurrency's stock is believed to be completed through the distribution and trading of stock on the blockchain application. The trading has made massive differences in the financial sector. The reason that crypto stock trade seems to be the future is that stock trading had middlemen that cryptocurrency has been able to eliminate. Peer trading and fees are also going to be cut out of the equation thanks to applications such as Ethereum. Since peer to peer training is free, there will be a better margin for those who are trading stock. It is also going to offer a new category for items that can be traded on a decentralized application. In the end, blockchain will be able to grow in shares that no one will be ready for.

- Ethereum's ecosystem will be increasing. The developers will be working on projects that they are excited to release to the public. Some of the projects will be titled Colony, Augur, and Weifund.

Augur: you will find that this is a dapp application that will assist you in predicting what the market will do along with predicting what is tradable and what the outcome will be depending on the network that you are using instead of depending on a central authority to figure it out for you.

Weifund: another dapp application that helps with crowdfunding campaigns. Whenever you use Weifund, you will manage your own campaigns as well as look at other campaigns. As you go about investing in these campaigns, you will receive shares and tokens that can then be moved across the exchange.

Colony: with this dapp, you will create a decentralized organization. There will be people around the world that will work together on projects so that they are rewarded based on their contributions.

A transaction volume vs. the market cap: how many transactions that occur will depend on how high the price of ether is since the nodes on the network will be rewarding the validation of transactions.

Whenever Ethereum was first released, it started

confirming 15,000 transactions a day. It is predicted that the number of transactions happening will continue to rise as the platform continues to evolve and dapps continue to increase.

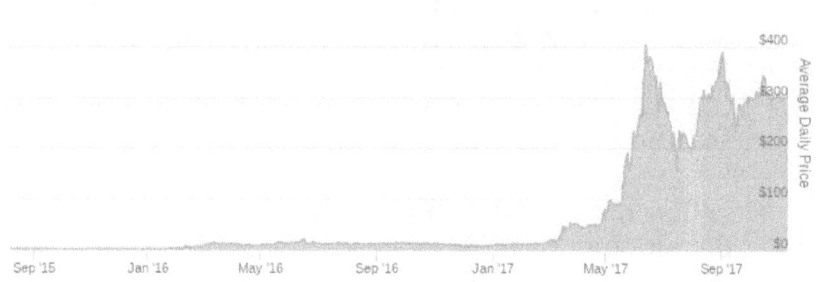

Exchange rates graph for ETH/USD (2015 - 2017)

Ether's market cap will be worth one hundred and ninety million dollars. But, the amount of ether that is available will be based on the number of applications that the platform will have for a short period of time. Whenever you look at the perspective of a market cap, then it will seem high, and there has to be a decline in the future. But, there is speculation about the value of the drivers for the market cap. These drivers will be the fundamental analysis of how much ether is currently on the platform.

Inflationary design: the last driver for ether's value drive will be inflationary design. The creator of Ethereum first started out on his quest; there was a model of inflation for ether. But, the new distribution system for ether on the network is also going to go up. The background for this made it to where ether was considered a product that would facilitate transactions that have to be done on the system. Whenever the price of ether goes up, then the way that the platform performs will be disrupted.

If the price of ether goes up, then it is not going to be an investment asset anymore which will end up meaning that there will be an adverse effect on Ethereum's future development. When you look at the current policy of how ether will be distributed and you will realize that what will happen is not clear enough for you to understand what will happen. But, there will be signs of inflation that you will see at a low level; there is the possibility that it will vanish altogether. However, it is uncertain what will happen with the future distribution of ether and how the potential risk will be outweighed by the other drivers

In the end, there are users who think that Ethereum will be the leading platform for most investment opportunities. When you observe the fundamentals, then you will notice that the market cap is set at three hundred and fifty million; and, with how the current market is going, it will seem like the cap is set too high.

While time moves on, you will begin to see that the Ethereum projects will get enough funding because of the demand for ether which will end up leveling out the market cap. But, on the other hand, you can see that projects on Ethereum that are still in their early stages are only going to go up from here as long as the market continues to stay open. But, as blockchain gains more momentum, Ethereum will be released entirely and will take a massive hit in its investments.

It is easy to get lost in every update that comes, but you cannot allow yourself to because it will cause you to lose focus on your investments and you may end up spending more than you are willing to spend. Finances will hold some risk of degree, however, with Ethereum it is well worth the risk.

When it comes to investing with Ethereum, you will follow the steps listed below.

1. Create an ethereum wallet. The wallet that you create will be where all of your ether will go so that you can send out payments as well as the received hem. Sadly, when you look at ethereum, you will notice that since it is still a new platform, it may be difficult to find online wallets that are user-friendly.

Some users will use Ethereum and can testify that ether wallets can be made out of an online wallet generator that will give you public and private keys so that you can access your wallet without anyone else getting into it.

My ether wallet is a program that will enable you to print out your wallet and keep it in a safe place. It is recommended that you download the JSON file and place it in various locations so that you have access to it in the event that something happens.

As new transactions are created, your private key will have to be put into the file so that you can show that you are who you say you are.

2. You will need to obtain ether. You can exchange money for ether, or you can mine it. When you are buying ether, you can use shapeshift.io. This is a user-friendly site that will make it so that you do not have to register with them. You will have the option of switching between thirty-two different cryptocurrencies without any problem occurring on your end. But, you may find that you have an issue with some of the cryptocurrencies because there are not enough people who use them. So, purchasing them is not going to do anything for you but waste your time and your money.

One of the things that you will need to keep in mind is that no matter what cryptocurrency you choose, there will be a deposit box and a receiving box. As you place your public address into Ethereum, you will be agreeing to their terms before clicking start.

Now that you have done that, you will get a deposit from the system to make sure that you can send and receive coins. It is only going to take you a few minutes before you see your balance go up in your wallet. When you choose to mine with Ethereum, you must have a GPU card in the machine that you are using.

One of the more natural ways to mine is to go to what is

called a cloud mining contract and purchase it. This agreement will enable you to mine ether on the Ethereum system.

It is recommended that you use Genesis Mining and you can find out more information on them by going to their website.

http://bitcoinpassiveincome.com/genesis-mining-review-get-89-roi-per-year/

3. Look at the balance in your wallet and send ether. When you want to look at your wallet's balance, you will click on "view wallet details," and you will be able to see every transaction that has taken place in your wallet.

When you want to send ether, it will be as simple as clicking on "send transaction" and entering the receiver's public key.

Now you are ready to invest with Ethereum!

There are other resources that you will have access to online so that you can find how other people have learned how to invest with Ethereum. It may appear that it is hard to invest, but if you follow these steps, you will do just fine. If you are still lost in investing with Ethereum, then you will want to ask someone who has been using Ethereum longer so that they can help you in a different way.

MATT COHEN

CHAPTER 6
MINING ETHER ON ETHEREUM

You do not have to buy ether if you do not want to. You can always mine it and here is how.

Put C++ visual on your computer

You will either be working with a 64-bit or a 32-bit computer. You will have to download the proper visual from Microsoft when you are downloading C++ to mine appropriately. If at all possible you will want to work with a 64-bit computer because the 32 system has some issues when you are mining ether. But, if that is all that you have to work with, you will have to be patient with the program as it works through its issues.

Install ethereum

The next step will be to download Mist. Mist will be your graphical interface that will be where your wallet is for ethereum. Mist is user-friendly and offers help through a browser application that you will want to get so that you can find other people who will be in a position to help you should you need help.

Get blockchain

This step will take a while for you to complete due to the fact that it will be where you download the blockchain onto your computer. The file that you will be downloading will be a ten-gigabyte file. So, if you start downloading this record, it is a good idea to find something else to do while it does what it needs to do.

Set up your wallet

Now will be a good time for you to set up your wallet. You have a lot of options when it comes to picking which wallet you can use. You will need to look at the security that the wallet has to offer as well as the benefits that you will receive from that wallet to choose the one that will be the one for you to use. Have a wallet is vital because it will be where all of your ether will be sent when you are rewarded for the work that you do.

Install Nvidia Cuda, CL SDK, or AMD

You will need to check your GPU before you can install the program that will be working off of the GPU. The application that you download will be based on your GPU's strength.

Install AlethOne Miner

You are most likely working as an individual so you will want to download AletheOne. AletheOne is the system that you are working on to allow you to mine. Remember that a 32-bit system will freeze and present other issues when it comes to mining so try and avoid them.

Wait for the DAG initialization

When AletheOne is done, you will have to wait for around ten minutes so that you can build a DAG. The DAG file will be stored on the computers RAM so that an algorithm can be created that is ASIC resistant.

Join a mining pool

The chances are that you are not going to be working in a warehouse that is full of GPU, so you will want to find a mining pool that will be right for you. This will go back to the competition that you read about earlier. You do not want to join a pool that is not going to make it to where you have to fight against too many miners. This will be because if there are other people that are more competent than you, you will be putting yourself in the position where you may not be getting rewards for the work that you do or, if you do get a reward, it is not going to be as big as it could be.

CHAPTER 7
ETHEREUM SMART CONTRACTS

Blockchain was first created to be used with bitcoin because it is the first cryptocurrency. But, when Ethereum came around, there was technology created that would allow for smart contracts to be created. Ethereum is the cryptocurrency that will focus on peer to peer transactions.

In this chapter, you will learn about how to create an Ethereum contract despite the blockchain that you are using because the process will be the same.

You are also going to learn how to analyze you are your contract so that you can ensure that it is written the way that you want it to be before it is placed on the blockchain to be executed.

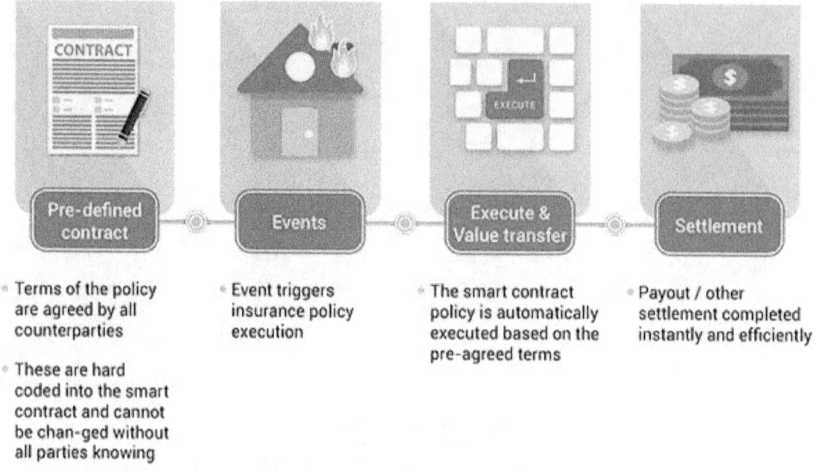

Example of smart contract in the insurance field

Definitions

There will be a few terms that you must know to deploy your contract to the blockchain for use.

Public key cryptography: the public key will be made up of a two-part system. The private key is an open key as well. Individuals will have to make a virtual signature that will mark all their blockchain work. It is vital that the users create backups of their keys since they are not going to be able to access their accounts without them. And, there is not going to be any way to access them externally.

Ethereum virtual machine: Smart contracts will be written with the blockchain infrastructure that is appropriate for that contract.

Dapp: this decentralized application will be used for smart contracts that are written and placed on the Ethereum marketplace. Dapp will run from a central location or Ethereum nodes.

Blockchain: this is a public ledger that will hold all the transactions done on a cryptocurrency network.

Ether: this is the digital currency used with Ethereum. Ether is referred to as ETH, and one ETH will be worth sixty-five cents in US dollars.

Starting your contract

It is not required, but when you are making your contract, you will be making your own Ethereum node, and it is recommended that you do so, even if you do not use it. As you use a node, you will have the power to connect to the entire Ethereum network. This will include the Ethereum tools of Java, C++, Haskell, and Python.
As of right now, the solidity tool is a programming language which will be the primary programming tool. It will be the ethereum version of JavaScript while using extensions of .se or .sol. A compiler is also going to be required. Ensure that you have the C++ library so that you can have all of the tools that you need to write your contract. Downloading C++ will make it to where you do not have to install solc. There is an alternative that you can use, and that will be a web version that you can find at etherchain.org, or you can use Cosmo. The last thing that you will need is web3.ja; this is an API application that will create dapp. When you have a solidity contract compiled it will be sent to the network. From there, the contract will be recalled with web3.js. So, now, you will have the option of building web applications that will interact with your contracts appropriately.

If you are interested in taking advantage of a framework that already exists, then you will need to use the distributed application framework called Truffle. Truffle will be the recommended choice when it comes to using a basic program that you will understand while allowing for a more significant emphasis to be placed on the individual code. If you do not want to use your own node, then you will need to use blockapps.net. This is another API that will give you the effect of working with a node for testing purposes without having to work with your own node.

There will be specifics in contracts that will vary greatly which means that there will be variables that must be inside of each contract in one form or another. Take for example that if an event occurs then the result will be kept in a log that will create an agreement, but it is not going to affect how the deal acts. At the same time, there is a function that will alter the yes and no state of the contract through the modification of the values that were put into place before the contract was activated. It is because of this function that the move will be moved from one account to another when conditions are met.

The contracts address will be will determine the location of your wallet and if the contract can access your wallet through its unique address which will keep the creator address separate from the wallet address. The next variable will be the size of the contract; the smaller the contract, the better it will run. On top of that, a smart contract will be able to pull data from the oracle by using a public variable that will end up determining if the data needs to be consulted or not and where that information will be coming from.

Other things you will want to consider

As you are writing out contracts, you will need to look at the information that you are working with so that you can make sure that you are storing all the data in the contract so that the terms can be met. You will have a list of items that will end up determining the overall structure of the file that you are modifying. This data is usually going to be stored in a 2-xn mapping sequence. N will be the number of transaction that will be finished along with the specific details that are tied to each transaction.

As you keep the outcome in mind, you will need to include the definition for two different struts. The first one will include information for the person who started the transaction, and that means that the amount of the transaction will be in this strut. The second strut will hold the data for the storage and any information that is needed for mapping the contract as it should be. It is with this strut that you will outline the database that you are working with so that it will automatically label the contracts based on the template that you have created.

Now that you have gotten the template creation out of the way, you will define the functions that will be executed on a regular basis and the prompts that will allow it to carry out the tasks that happen daily. The proper transactions will be sent to the owner of the contract. This idea was first proposed to include the limits that the transaction will add, the contracts fund account, and the stipulations that will apply.

The investor's transactions will be identified by a unique ID that will be stored in the space that has already been set aside for that record, and that has to do with that contract. This area will have been set aside beforehand by the system so that all the results from the contract are kept in the same place. If there is a time limit that is placed on the transaction, then the final deal will be generated. This will then trigger the last action which is often referred to as the suicide action so that the contract cannot be rerun.

It is now that the user will have the opportunity to figure out what they want to do with the funds that they have gotten. These results will then be tested after the contract has been uploaded. A dummy contract will list you in the investor category. You will be required to go through the motions of interacting with the agreement to make sure that it will react in the way that you want it to.

Proper execution

As you saw earlier, Truffle will be the programming process that will make your contract more manageable if you are not comfortable putting all your information together before you test your code first. To help the writing process, Truffle will check the scenarios in the contracts through a Java framework. You should keep in mind that the transaction will take around ten seconds to be verified and that is only if everything in the contract is written correctly. It is vital that you are taking the time into account as you test your code for your contract.

You must have access to the window on the console you are writing your smart contract on, so a new node can be created before the truffle program is opened. When you use the command, it will deploy truffle and cause a spawn to occur in the basics of the init for the smart contract. The code can be tested through the compiling all the code and checking it for errors and deployment errors.

What happens next

Once the contract's code has been written, it must be formatted so that it can be placed on the blockchain; and you will do this by using an online compiler for solidity found at etherchain.org/solc. At the point in time that your code has been formatted, you will upload the contract by paying the small amount of ether to receive a signature box where you will insert your private key, marking the contract as yours. You are then going to receive the results through an ABI and the blockchain address where the data is now going to be stored for the rest of that contracts life.

After everything has been compiled and updated, the contract needs to be deployed through truffle. You have to open the truffle console and access a new directory by inserting the init command. A new index will be created, and it will place an extension of .sol on the contract. You are now going to enter config/app.son so that you can add the contract to the space that has been provided for it. All you will need to do now is restart your program and run the tesrpc command so that truffle is deployed at the root level. But your contract should be live on the blockchain.

Once the contract has been created, then there has to be a user interface formed that will make it to where you will interact with the arrangement in real time. The dapp will be inside of a database that contains an HTML based front end, and it will be linked directly to the Ethereum platform. If you are using truffle, then the dapp will tie it into a complete network with CDN access. Dapp's UI will be created in a way that is similar to how websites will be designed.

There will be different frameworks that will help in the creation of your dapp so that it is easier for you to deal with. As you saw above, the truffle will be a tool that you will have the option of using, but it is not going to only take that you can use. You are also going to be able to use Embark; but, the truffle will be the most straightforward development tool that you can use in the creation of your dapp.

When you use truffle, you will be creating a smart contract. But, it is vital to know that there are other options that you can use so that you are making an informed decision as to which application is best for you.

Truffle will be an application that will do most of the work for you when you are working with dapp and smart contracts.

The Embark application will aid in deploying your contracts so that they are available in the JS code of your choice. Embark is also going to make it to where changes will be tracking all of the updates to your contract. Should this occur, embark will redeploy your contract automatically and dapp as needed.

Dapp creation

When dapp is created, you will want to use truffle since it will compile your UI automatically once it has been established. The truffle director has to be labeled app so that the next time that it is run, it will compile the contact information. It will also collect any new changes into the build folder where it can be called upon in case of emergencies with the truffle application.

To get started the directory has to be labeled as an app so that it can find the background images and the JavaScript code that will be tied to the stylesheets and indexes. Depending on what you are needed, you will have the option of adding the code directly into the file that already exists so that you can obtain the front-end UI option which will cause your contract to be up and running in no time. When you open the app.js file, there will be a section that will provide you with a greeting from truffle in the developer console. When you open this console, there will be a list of active commands.

While thinking about commands, you will need to create a function that will have the ability to be accessed every time that a page loads. To do this, you will need a window added by using the code window.onload in the app.js file. If you do this correctly, there will be an assortment of account details that will be shown in the console browser. Finally, you will use a test. Conference.js function so that you can make sure that the output is working as you want it to. Your output should be the balance amount, and this balance will increase after the situation is deferred.

After the app.js has been created along with the index.html so that it will meet your needs, you will test the results with your node or a sample node that will give you results in real time. Note: the results are not going to be prepared relatively quickly. You will want to use the following code so that you can ensure that it will work correctly.

geth --rpc --rpcaddr="0.0.0.0" --rpccorsdomain="*" --mine --unlock='0 1'verbosity=5 --maxpeers=0 --minerthreads='4' --networkid '12345' --genesis testgenesis.json

There will be two new accounts that will be labeled zero and one. You have to understand that you will need both accounts so that a password can be created for each report separately which will end up generating a json test-genesis file that will be founded under alloc on the account where your ether costs are kept. Lately, you will add the results to your truffle application so that you can recompile the contract and deploy the results once more.

There is an option that you will be able to use to generate a UI to use with any dapp that will be created by silent cicero. You can find this application at dapp-builder.metor.com. It is this tool that will be used in creating HTML code you can later modify for your contracts written out on solidity, web3.js or jQuery. It is not going to run as smoothly as you will want it to, but if you are not comfortable with your skill level when it comes to going through the process on their own. The UI that follows will use the same steps like the ones that you have already seen above. If it does not, then there is a secondary version that is usually going to be easier for you to use in finding a solution to your problem.

It is at this point in time that the contract will be written, but you are not going to be done just yet. You have to analyze the agreement. When you examine it, you will ensure that the deal is written correctly and does not need to be tweaked.

Looking at the variables that are located at the top of your contract, they will look like this:

Address public organizer;
Mapping (address => uint) public registrants Paid;
Uint public nonresistant;
Uint public quota;

Address: since this is the first variable in your contract, it will be your wallet address. The address will be set when the constructor which will be called conference (). But, in most cases, the contract will name it the owner.

Uint: you will see that this will be the unsigned integer. There has to be space on the blockchain; this is why you will need to try and keep everything as small as possible.

Public: there will be a variable called from outside of the contract that you write. When working with a private modifier, it will be called on by the agreement. But, if you try and call upon a variable from web3.js then you have to ensure that the variable is set to public.

Mapping and Arrays: there will be varying levels of support for the arrays and mapping like (address => uint) that will be used by solidity. It is also going to write an address out as registrants paid []. These mappings will hold a smaller footprint. Therefore, the mapping will be used in storing the registrant that paid for them so that their funds are available later.

Extra about addresses: this is a client node that will hold information about your account. Whenever you begin your test, then there will be an array of ten addresses that are available.

Your first account will be labeled zero, and it will be the default for any transaction when the state has not already been specified.

Organizer address vs. Contract address: your contract will have its own contract address once it is deployed and this address will be different from the organizer's address. This address will be able to be accessed through your solidity contract. It will be used in your refund ticket function which will be in the contract as address = this;

Suicide, a good thing in Solidity: should any funds be sent to your contract; they will be held by the agreement itself. With the destroy function, the resources will be released to the owner of the deal. Should this not be put into place, then the funds would end up being tied up, and no one would ever be able to access them. So, it is vital that you include a suicide method in your contract so that if your contract dies, you will be able to collect the funds.

However, if you simulate another party of the contract, then you will have the option of using another address that will be different from the accounts array. Therefore, to buy a ticket, you will have to buy it through this function.

Conference. buy Ticket ({
From: accounts [1], value: some_ticket_price_integer});

Some Function calls can be transactions: functions will be able to change the state of your contract, and these deals will have a specific sender as well as a value that will be placed inside of the curly braces. The funds are then going to be transferred to the wallet's address. So, with solidity, you will have the option of retrieving values through the msg. sender and Ms. Value where the functions for the solidity are stored.

Function buy Ticket () public {
...
registrants Paid [msg. sender] = msg. value;
...
}

Events: events will be optional when you are going through the process to write your contract. Deposits will be set to be sent inside of the agreement to be logged by the virtual machine. But, they are not going to do anything; it is just going to be good practice for you so that you can keep track of all your transactions that have happened already.

MATT COHEN

CHAPTER 8
PROGRAMMING WITH ETHEREUM

Smart contracts are ideal for ethereum since they work on a prominent level that will maintain the space in the virtual machine bytecode before it lets it go to the blockchain so that it can be executed. As you saw in the last chapter, most contracts are written by solidity; but some will be written by LLL, mutant, and serpent. You will find that no matter what programming language you use with ethereum, they will be part of Python or JavaScript due to the fact that they are two of the most commonly used for programming

Research has been done in creating a new language for ethereum that is called Viper. Viper will be derived from python; however, it is not going to work outside of ethereum. This means that if you want to write other codes, you will be required to use python instead of viper. Python will be accepted in almost any form.

Contracts that are written on the ethereum blockchain will be stored where they can be examined by the public. But, one of the disadvantages you will notice about ethereum is that it will have performance issues when it comes to the nodes because they are will be trying to calculate the contract in real time, and this causes the performance speeds to be reduced.

Ethereum engineers have been working on sharding calculations, but a solution has not been found yet. In 2016, a new protocol was put into place so that twenty-five transactions could be done per second. Later in the same year, the creator of ethereum said that they had to increase Ethereum's scalability so that it was more efficient for its users.

The blockchain platform will have several different processes that will be used to make the platform tamper-proof.

CHAPTER 9
PROBLEMS YOU MAY RUN INTO WITH ETHEREUM

No matter what it is, when something is new, there will be things that will stop the development process. These problems will hinder the users from being able to control the platform and its software. However, if you understand what is blocking you, then you will have the ability to avoid it and continue to use the system as if these issues did not even exist.

1. The first roadblock you will notice is Ethereum's scalability. Because of the claims that are often repeated about mainstream payment network process, there will be around two thousand transactions completed per second, but the Ethereum network is only going to have the ability to do seven. But, you will have the option of changing the limit parameters so that you can complete more transactions a second. There is always the possibility that Ethereum will get too big and it will force users to run full nodes. But, if a whole node is being relegated, then there will be some businesses that will be the only ones who can afford the resources that are needed to run that node. So, this means that you do not have to download blockchain for some of the Ethereum tasks.

Therefore, the most significant problem will be the design of blockchain that will help to maintain the security that Ethereum offers so that it can ensure the maximum size of the most potent nodes that will work in supporting the high number of transactions that are being completed.

A few more problems that can cause scaling issues are:

A) How many users are on the network.

B) Users that are using specialized hardware or unspecialized hardware. When the equipment is specialized, it will be more powerful than an unspecialized device.

C) The probability that most users will be using hardware that is unspecialized.

D) There are some transactions where blocks will require fifty-one percent of the network's hash power so that it can reverse a transaction. But, the solution is that deals will pay small fees so that there is a lower level of security. This will mean that users will need to avoid situations where if there is an attacker on the network, they will be able to perform an attack on a small number of transactions in an effort to make a profit.

E) Most situations will work to keep up the properties that will aid in generalizing the account's blockchain. However, the answers will be specific to the digital currency along with the domain's registrations or other specialized cases that will be acceptable.

2. Time stamping is also going to be an issue with Ethereum. Most of the time a block will be created every ten minutes. But, when a block is built every day, the system will be too slow, and if blocks are created too fast, then the platform will become overwhelmed, and there will be issues with how

the platform will perform. This is why there is a "happy medium" so that the blocks can be created in a timely manner without messing up the performance of the system.

So, the most significant issue will be a distribution creation problem that will involve the incentive-compatible system. This will require that there is an overlay on top of the block or the chain so that the time is kept accurately.

Extra time stamping problems will be:

1. Any user that is using a clock for standard distributions around what is considered the real-time that will be deviated by twenty seconds.

2. The fact that two nodes are never within twenty seconds from each other in terms of the amount of time it takes for the message to originate from one node while another node receives it.

3. There can be solutions that will rely on the existing nodes. But, this practice will require proof of stake or for a non-Sybil token to be enforced.

4. There have been some users that have suggested that the system will provide the time that is at least a hundred and twenty seconds less than the system's internal clock. This will be around ninety-nine percent of the nodes that are participating causing them to do what is required of them. Note: this will mean that the system has to be self-consistent within a hundred and ninety seconds.

5. The system is then going to exist without there being any need for proof of work from the system's users.

6. The external system will rely on the new system that has been created. This means that it will stay secure from an attacker that is wanting to control

twenty-five percent of the nodes no matter what the incentive is.

You will find other things that will cause you to have trouble with using the Ethereum platform. The developers of the system are working hard to get rid of the barriers and make the system more user-friendly. But, it is not going to fix the problem overnight. Sometimes there will be problems with the system itself, and the developers are not always going to be able to fix those.

Users are always going to find problems that developers miss. So, if you find a problem, you will need to report it so that it can be added to the list of issues that the developers know about and have to fix. When you report problems, you will be helping to create a better system not only for you but for other users as well.

As you already know, problems that are found need to be reported since the developers are trying to fix issues that are informed by other users. You have to keep in mind that the developers are human too and they will have their own life that they will need to deal with on top of doing their job. There is a lot of code that makes up the Ethereum platform, and, that is a lot of code to go through so that every issue can get fixed properly. There are bound to be issues that will occur and stick around for a while. So, have faith in the developers because they will get through the problems that are reported, and you will notice that the platform will be more efficient thanks to users like you!

CHAPTER 10
TIPS AND TRICKS FOR USING ETHEREUM

Platforms like ethereum will be hard to use, and you are most likely going to get frustrated. But, when you have the proper tips and tricks that will make using the system that much easier. The more that you use the system, the faster it will be for you to find ways around issues like we talked about in an earlier chapter. So, take the tips and tricks that the ethereum users have to offer so that you can avoid some of the mistakes that they have already made.

Your password

You have heard it a thousand times over, and you will hear it again here. **You have to have a secure password!** It is rare to find someone who will use a secure password, and with a little digging you can usually figure out what their password is so that you can hack into your account. Therefore, with a secure password, you will be keeping your cryptocurrency safe and ensuring that you do not lose your coins.

Think of your password as a shield for your account. It will keep attackers out of your account, so the stronger your password, the stronger your protection will be. And, when dealing with your crypto assets, you will want a secure password just like you would want a secure password for your bank account.

In the event that you do not know what a secure password will consist of, here is a guideline.

1. Letters

2. Numbers

3. Symbols

4. And must be at least sixteen characters long.

Not all passwords will require sixteen characters, however, the longer that the password is, the less likely it is that someone will be able to hack it and get into your cryptocurrency wallet. Long passwords may be hard for you to remember, so it is recommended that you write it down to be able to remember it. There are also going to be tools available for you to find online that will generate passwords that will be memorable and strong. But, do not use a password manager or else someone will have the ability to find the password if they hack into your computer rather than attempt to hack into your account. Password managers will be great if you are using passwords for everyday things, but as was just stated, it will be easy for someone to get all of your passwords just by hacking into your computer. Then you are not only going to lose your crypto assets; you will lose your identity as well.

Encrypt your wallet

Wallets for cryptocurrency are sensitive applications that will store the details of your digital currency funds. Every wallet will offer you a different level of security, but they all strive to provide a high level of protection for their users. In the event that you are in a hurry to create a wallet, you are most likely going to want to use *My ether wallet* because it is the first ethereum wallet that was designed and it will be the one that is trusted the most as a highly functional wallet. But, it does not matter how secure your password is for your wallet, it is not going to be able to stop the hackers that use keylogging and other advanced attacks to gain your information.

Sync your wallet

It will benefit you if you think of your wallet as your bank account. There will be funded in your wallet, and you are not going to want anyone to get ahold of them. So, you will want to find a program online that will provide you with the option of backing up your wallet. It is a wise idea to back up your wallet. There are some programs that will offer you the option of syncing once and then the program automatically syncing whenever there are changes to your account. When you back up your wallet, you will be saving your account from system failures and crashes. But, do not just back up your wallet, back up your keys as well. Backing up your keys will make it to where you will have the ability to get back into your wallet. And, your keys are not going to be able to be retrieved externally once they have been lost, this is why you will need to have them backed up elsewhere. It is not a bad idea to put your wallet on an external hard drive, on a flash drive, and even printing it out. You can also convert it into a json file so that it is saved offline.
Some backups that you can use are :

1. Backup wallet.dat

2. Bip 32 wallet

Use multi-signatures

Having multiple signatures means that there will be several people in your wallet. But, you do not have to have someone else on your crypto wallet if you do not want there to be. You can use another device of yours, as long as it is not the primary device that you use for your ethereum account. But, if you trust someone with your digital currency, then you will be able to use a business partner or your spouse. Really, you can use anyone that you trust enough to not steal your currency. How many signatures are required to complete a transaction will be determined by how many signatures you set up when you first set up your wallet. There will be a few web wallets that will offer you the option of using multiple signatures in an effort to make it to where there is less fraud of your digital currency.

Some wallets are:

1. Blocktrail

2. Coinbase

CHAPTER 11
THE ETHEREUM ECOSYSTEM

Ethereum's technologies will make up its ecosystem. Every part of the ecosystem will be a piece that is required to make sure that Ethereum works the way that it is supposed to.

Clients and wallets

1. Parity: Rust implementation

2. Keep Key: wallet – hardware

3. My ether wallet: wallet – online

4. Jaxx: wallet – online

5. Mist: wallet – desktop

6. Cpp: implementation of C++

7. Gerth : Go implementation

8. Ledfer nano s: wallet – hardware

9. Hyper ledger burro: monax creation for the virtual machine in go

Decentralized application

1. Slock: a program that uses smart locks for communication purposes

2. Music: copyrights and royalties are kept on the blockchain in an effort to reduce piracy and ensure that artists are getting paid.

3. Digital signatures: signatures that will provide proof of existence by any document that is used by the Luxembourg Stock exchange.

4. Digix: a platform tied to a digital token that is backed by gold.

5. Identity system: they locate where Ethereum will ensure that the platform is secure enough to use the internet via uPort.

6. Digital tokens: fiat digital currency. The Spanish bank proposed the idea when Ethereum came around.

7. Interactive guide: you can find this guide for IoT and other topics such as using Bluetooth and other communication chips.

CHAPTER 12
BUYING ETHEREUM

If you do not want to mine ether, you can purchase it. When you decide to purchase your first Ethereum, you will want to follow a specific set of steps to buy ether, and ether will be a vital part of what the Ethereum platform is built on just as bitcoin is an essential part of the Bitcoin platform.

1. Purchase ether through Coinbase

    1. Create a Coinbase account

    2. Insert your payment method

    3. Select how much ether you want to buy under buy/ sell

    4. Push purchase

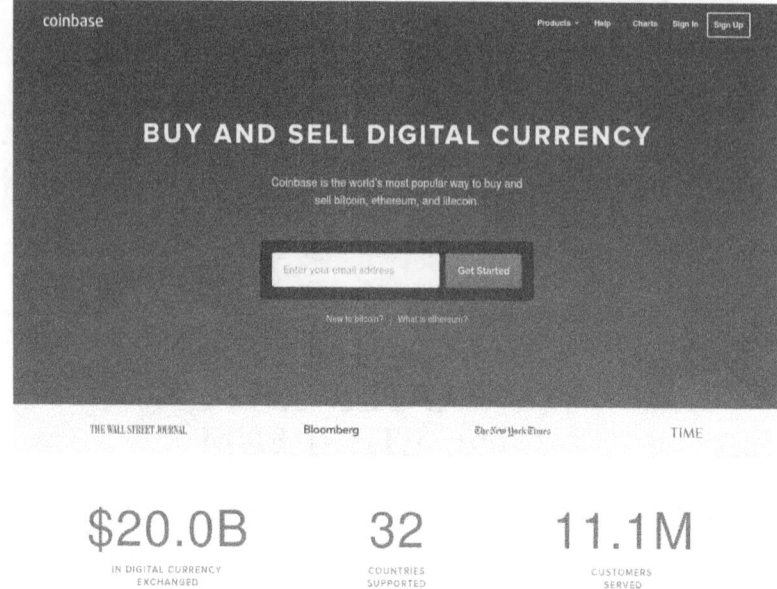

A screenshot of coinbase.com

Coinbase will charge you 3.99% fee depending on the payment method that you are using. Credit cards will hold a higher transaction fee.

2. Cex.io is another way that you can buy ether. This website will have a higher exchange rate, but it will be tied to the total cost. This will save you from attempting to figure out what the exchange rate will be. While Coinbase may be better for you to use, cex.io will be available throughout the world.

   1. Make an account

   2. Insert your payment method

   3. Go to the buy or sell menu

4. Select the amount of ether you want to purchase

5. Buy your ether and enjoy it.

MATT COHEN

CHAPTER 13
ETHEREUM MILESTONES

There have been several types of prototypes that have been developed for ethereum. The ethereum foundation has used these prototypes to develop their proof of concept series. The last prototype that was allowed for beta testing was Olympic. Through trial and error, there were twenty-five thousand bugs that were found and fixed.

Frontier came after Olympic, and this was an experiment that was put into beta in the year 2015. Every ethereum launch has created a more stable platform that has changed and included updates that have worked in the prototypes. There have been a few changes that have affected how the platform works.

The most current prototype was Homestead, and it is considered to be the most stable prototype yet. Homestead improved the transaction process, enhanced security and cost of gas. There have been two more updates planned for Ethereum's future.

Ethereum's first upgrade was a metropolis, and this update was meant to reduce the complexity of the virtual machine while creating flexibility for how smart contracts are written. The screnity update did not come with any clear updates for ethereum, but it is believed that it fixed the algorithms that are used with ethereum in an effort to fix the sharding issues.

The DAO was created in 2016. The smart contracts would go through this decentralized system so that money could be raised in an effort to fund projects adequately. The DAO exploited somewhere around fifty million dollars in ether to an unknown entity. Because of this exploitation, a significant debate rose in the crypto community about if a hard fork should occur in an effort to recover the money. Since the discussion was so intense, that the community split in two. There were the people who liked the update and those who did not. Those who preferred to used ethereum from before the update were known as ethereum classics.

CHAPTER 14
SMART CONTRACT MYTHS

Smart contracts have not been around long, and to some, they are still hypothetical. Because of this, there have been some myths constructed about smart contracts. In this chapter, you will learn what these myths are and the truth so that you can better understand smart contracts.

Legally binding

Smart contracts will be automated for smaller processes; they are usually going to be tied to a contract that is legally binding; however, there is not going to be any legislation that will state smart contracts are legally binding anywhere in the world. So, smart contracts will be able to include a clause that will be similar to a traditional agreement. Take, for example; you want to sell a car that has a button you can push in the event that payments are not made. When this button is pushed, then the doors will be locked, and the owner is not going to be able to get into it until the payment is made. So, you can write out a contract that has this clause in it so that the person buying the car from you know all of the facts and is not going to be able to dispute them because they will be laid out in black and white. Plus, it is not going to leave any room for haggling.

But, this does not mean that there is not going to be anything that can be done about them. A digital signature that is tied to a smart contract will be considered an agreement. Therefore, the person that is responsible for their half of the deal will know what is required of them. And, there is not going to be any need for the courts to get involved.

Smart contracts and Ricardian contracts

Smart contracts will be able to supplement a Ricardian contract. However, they are not going to fit into the Ricardian definition. Ricardian contracts are verbal representations of a contract that will hold both parties liable to an agreement that was stated beforehand. The Ricardian process will be simplified thanks to smart contracts once the parameters and the variables are defined and identified. Ricardian contracts will usually require a few signatures, but a smart contract will excel and start tracking once the first name has been signed.

Smart contracts are like people – they can think and reason

Smart contracts will be binary codes, and they will determine the current state of the environment around the contract based on predetermined metrics. In the end, smart contracts are a piece of artificial intelligence that will work based off of predetermined events.

Useful for the financial sector
Using smart contracts will be most helpful in the financial sector. However, they will be able to be used in any sector that they have to be used in. Smart contracts will be limitless in what they will be able to be used for. Yes, they will be useful in the financial sector because they will be helpful when it comes to settlements and loans. Smart contracts will hold the information that the person with the investment will have. So, it will get rid of the need for duplicate paperwork to be printed out and possibly lost.

Useful for business

As you saw above, smart contracts will be able to be used in any sector. Businesses will be able to use smart contracts will be particularly useful when dealing with transactions for good and services. That way there is not going to be any need to haggle on price or any conditions about the sale. Just like you saw with the car example earlier, all of the requirements for the sale will be laid out, and there is not going to be any way for the buyer to say that they did not know that was a condition.

External factors
Using oracles is becoming more popular, but that does not mean that a smart contract will be able to use conditions that are already verified because there will be different shades of variance. Smart contracts will end up determining if a binary event has occurred. Adding different variables will make it to where two nodes will give you two different answers, and the entire thing will be thrown out as a result. This is something that you will have to deal with because every node will check the information that comes in through the oracles whenever it is pinged for information. There will be a ten-second delay between each node.

MATT COHEN

CONCLUSION

Thank you for making it through to the end of *Ethereum*, let's hope it was informative and able to provide you with all the tools you need to achieve your goals whatever it may be.

Now you will want to make an Ethereum account and start investing with Ethereum. As you have seen in this book, there are a lot of good things that will come from using Ethereum; especially since it will be the platform that will change the future of the financial sector.

There is no guarantee that the financial sector will be changed because of Ethereum, but there is not going to be the promise that Etherem will be around for an extended period of time. However, as Ethereum has proven, it seems like it will be around because it is continuing to evolve and adapted to the new technology.

You will find that investing with Ethereum will be a lot different than investing with bitcoin. Investing with Ethereum will give you more options for investing, and you will be able to do more with Ethereum.

The smart contracts that you will be able to work will make it so that you can get rid of judges and lawyers that way you can save more money on top of the money that you are already saving because you do not have to rent a building and get office supplies.

In the end, investing with Ethereum will be your choice, but if it was up to us, we would recommend that you invest in it!

Finally, if you found this book useful in any way, a review on Amazon is always appreciated!

Thank you and good luck!

OTHER BOOKS BY MATT COHEN

Bitcoin: Complete Guide to Mastering Bitcoin Mining, Trading, and Investing

Discover how YOU can make money with Bitcoin

Back in 2010 1 Bitcoin was valued $0.003. Since then its value has been radically increasing. In 2011 Bitcoin took parity with US Dollar, in 2013 it was worth 266$ (an astonishing increase of 26500%). 4 years later 1 Bitcoin was valued roughly 1000$. Because of this insane growth, Bitcoin has been defined as the new gold rush. Making money mining, trading or investing in Bitcoin is completely possible. You're missing a lot of opportunities if you still haven't jump on board, because overall Bitcoin value keeps increasing.

"As of October 2017 1 BITCOIN is valued $4.165".

Bitcoin is different from all the other currencies because no one can control it. Bitcoins are a digital currency exchanged between users through the net, they aren't printed by a central bank and can't be devalued. Thanks to its decentralized nature Bitcoin provides a lot of opportunity for people to profit. However, due to its seemingly complex and technical nature Bitcoin may seem difficult to understand for non-technical users.

Imagine if you could discover the exact tools savvy investors use to make a lot of money trading, mining and investing in Bitcoins.

In this book you'll find everything you need to know about the Bitcoin world and the blockchain technology. You'll discover all the websites and softwares that will give you the ability to earn money trading and investing in bitcoins, and all the tools and platforms you can use to mine bitcoins for a profit. This is an in-depth guide on cryptocurrency and bitcoin, but you'll be easily able to understand it even if you're a non-technical user.

What you'll discover:
- What Is a Bitcoin And How Does It Work
- Everything You Need To Start Mining Bitcoin For Profit
- How To Make Money Quickly Using Bitcoin Mining Platforms
- How To Avoid Losing Money With The Mining Profitability Calculator (100% Risk-Free)
- Trusted Platforms To Start Trading Bitcoin For Profit
- What Drives Bitcoin Price, And How To Take Advantage Of It
- A Scam Test To Discover If A Bitcoin Service Isn't

Legitimate Before Losing Money
- The Best Bitcoin Wallets For Computers And Smartphones
- 10 Important Rules To Keep Your Bitcoins Safe
- And Much, Much More

Don't miss the Bitcoin opportunity!

"Bitcoin" by Matt Cohen is available at Amazon.

Blockchain: Complete Guide To Understanding The Blockchain Technology Revolution And The Future Of Money

Discover The Technology That Will Change Our Financial System Forever

The blockchain technology is probably the greatest human invention after the internet. Simply put, the blockchain technology is a form of a distributed ledger that is decentralized and public and can record transactions with a very high level of security.

All the records in the blockchain are called blocks, and each of them is linked to the previous one with a hash pointer and is securely stored with cryptography. This technology is revolutionary because every transaction is recorded across a network of multiple computers in the net. This way, no record can be altered or modified without changing the other blocks.

Since the blockchain technology is so decentralized, it is free from control or influence of any central authority. Even the founder or developer of a blockchain cannot change the records without the consent of or notice to all the other users. The blockchain technology is still in its early days, but it's already clear that it has the potential to change our financial system forever.

"The Blockchain Will Do To The Financial System What The Internet Did To Media".

Imagine if you could discover the ins and outs of the blockchain technology and all the ways to take advantage of it. Remember, learning and investing in blockchain today might just be the best decision that you can make.

In this comprehensive guide you'll find everything you need to know about the Blockchain technology, Blockchain based applications and interesting future developments. This is an in-depth guide on the blockchain technology, but you'll be easily able to understand it even if you're a non-technical user.

What you'll discover:
- What Is The Blockchain Technology And Exactly How Does It Work
- Real World Examples Of The Blockchain Technology
- How To Hack A Blockchain Network With The 51% Attack
- 5 Proven Ways To Profit From Cryptocurrencies

- The History Of The Blockchain Technology
- The Real Pros And Cons Of The Blockchain Technology
- 8 Core Strategies To Make Money Trading Cryptocurrencies (Every Investor Should Know These)
- The Common Mistakes Beginner Traders Make And How To Avoid Them
- Interesting Future Developments Of The Blockchain Technology
- How The Blockchain Technology Will Change Our Financial System Forever
- And Much, Much More

Take advantage of the revolution!

"Blockchain" by Matt Cohen is available at Amazon.

www.ingramcontent.com/pod-product-compliance
Lightning Source LLC
Chambersburg PA
CBHW070316230526
45470CB00002B/906